Artists at Work
Metals

Cheryl Jakab

Smart Apple Media

Smart Apple Media
2140 Howard Drive West
North Mankato
Minnesota 56003

First published in 2006 by
MACMILLAN EDUCATION AUSTRALIA PTY LTD
627 Chapel Street, South Yarra, Australia 3141

Visit our Web site at www.macmillan.com.au

Associated companies and representatives throughout the world.

Library of Congress Cataloging-in-Publication Data

Jakab, Cheryl.
    Metals / by Cheryl Jakab.
    p. cm.—(Artists at work)
    Includes index.
    ISBN-13: 978-1-58340-778-3
    1. Art metal-work—Juvenile literature. I. Title.

NK6404.2.J25 2006
739—dc22   2005057942

Edited by Sam Munday
Text and cover design by Karen Young
Page layout by Karen Young
Photo research by Jes Senbergs
Illustrations by Ann Likhovetsky

Printed in USA

Acknowledgments

The author would like to acknowledge and thank all the working artists and hobbyists who have been quoted, appear, or assisted in creating this book.

The author and the publisher are grateful to the following for permission to reproduce copyright material:

Cover photograph: A welder using a torch on cast bronze models of a horse sculpture, courtesy of Sheldan Collins/CORBIS.

Artlegends.com, p. 24 (top); James Binnion, p. 23; Coo-ee Picture Library, pp. 10, 20; Corbis, pp. 8, 9, 12 (both), 13, 14, 15, 16 (both), 17, 19, 21, 26; Getty Images, pp. 4 (left), 5, 18; Henry Moore Foundation, pp. 11, 22; Istockphoto, p. 4 (top right); Photodisc, pp. 4 (bottom right), 25; Photos.com, p. 6 (both); Society of American Silversmiths, p. 24 (bottom).

While every care has been taken to trace and acknowledge copyright, the publisher tenders their apologies for any accidental infringement where copyright has proved untraceable. Where the attempt has been unsuccessful, the publisher welcomes information that would redress the situation.

Please note

Contents

Glossary words

When a word is printed in **bold**, you can look up its meaning in the Glossary on page 31.

Metal artists

Look at these different artworks made by metal artists. Metal artists are people who design and make artworks in metal. Techniques used by metal artists include hammering, casting, etching, and joining. Metals are used by artists to create a wide variety of items including:

⊙ This sculpture is made entirely from metal coat hangers.

▶ fine silver, gold, and **titanium** jewelry

▶ precious silver and gold objects such as bowls, cups, and masks

▶ giant aluminum, iron, steel, and bronze sculptures

▶ iron and steel towers and bridges

▶ wrought iron furniture

▶ gold and silver medallions and coins

▲ Iron is often used to make huge metal artworks.

◀ Gold coins can be decorated with different designs.

 Some metal artists melt metal in order to work with it.

Using metal

Metals used by artists are divided into:

- precious metals, such as gold
- base metals, such as iron
- **alloys**, which are mixtures of metals such as bronze, steel, and pewter

In this book, you will find the answers to these questions and more:

- What do you need to know about metals to use them creatively?
- How do metals help the artist express ideas?
- What is it that metal artists like about metal as a **medium** for art?
- What do you need to do to work as a metal artist?

The Artist Speaks

"I like the way silver and gold hold intricate and delicate shapes while retaining a perfect surface."
Pam Brittain, silver worker

Metals are a group of strong, durable materials that have a smooth surface when polished. Metals are malleable, which means they can be worked into almost any shape. This allows them to be pressed when cold, and molded when hot. Metals are also reusable—they can be shaped, reshaped, then melted down to be used over again. The alloys of metals have different **properties** to the pure metals that go into them.

▼ Bronze (made by mixing copper and tin) is a very hard metal.

Properties of metal

Metals are a group of **chemicals** that are:

- solid at normal temperatures (except for **mercury**)
- easily mixed together when heated
- able to conduct heat and electricity
- shiny or **lustrous** when polished
- in the form of a **crystalline** structure when solid

► Pure copper is soft.

6

Characteristics of metal

Metal	Source	Properties	Melting point temperature (degrees Farenheit/°F)
aluminum	found as oxide in **bauxite ore**	• a soft powder in pure form • can be very strong when combined with other metals	1,220°F (660°C)—pure form 3,632°F (over 2,000°C)—aluminum oxide alloy
brass	alloy of copper and zinc	• does not rust easily • can be worked without melting first	depends on alloy mixture
bronze	alloy of copper and tin	• brown-yellow color • harder than copper • does not rust easily	depends on alloy mixture
copper	found in a range of mixed ores	• orange-pink color • a soft metal • resists corrosion	1,981°F (1,083°C)
gold	found in quartz veins or sedimentary deposits as pure gold	• the softest metal • does not rust easily • always shiny	1,947°F (1,064°C)
iron	found in iron ores such as magnetite and hematite	• silver-gray color • hard, but bendable	2,777°F (1,525°C)
lead	found all over the world as a compound in an ore called galena	• softest and weakest of the commonly used metals • poisonous	622°F (328°C)
silver	mostly found mixed with ores, but can also be found in pure form	• shiny white metal • soft and easy to work	1,764°F (962°C)
steel	alloy of iron, with up to 1.7 percent carbon and other metals	• very hard • can only be worked when hot	depends on alloy mixture
titanium	found in **igneous** rocks and their sediments, not as the pure metal	• silver-gray color • strong and light • does not rust easily	3,362°F (1,850°C)

Metal work

Artists working with metals make use of the special qualities of each metal. The smooth surface of stainless steel, the glint of gold, and the strength of bronze can all be used by the artist. Precious metals such as gold and silver are not only the most costly, they are also the softest. They are therefore used for small but valuable items such as jewelry.

The base metals (copper, tin, lead, and iron) and their alloys (bronze, brass, and pewter) are cheaper. Each metal has its own advantages and disadvantages. Iron, the most widely used metal, is strong enough to make large structures but rusts. Steel does not rust but is harder to work.

◀ Molten metal can be used to make new metal artworks.

8

Working with metal

Metal artists use different hammers, cutters, heaters, and molds for each type of metal. Some objects are cast in one piece and others need to be joined together. Types of joints used by metal workers include tying, **riveting**, and **welding**.

Welding

The oldest form of welding is called hammer welding. This is a process where the ends of two metal pieces are joined by being heated. They are then hammered together while still hot. Hammer welding is still used today by many metal workers. Welding can now also be done using modern tools and methods such as torches and **arc welding**. These tools can heat metals to higher temperatures.

⬇ Welding metal creates a bright and dangerous light.

"When arc welding I can pour metal into the gap in a sculpture to build up shape. I can then grind the product to refine that shape."
Ferenc Jakab, metal sculptor

9

Metal artists today

Metal artists use traditional techniques with new metals when they become available. They also constantly explore new ways to use traditional metals.

New metals, traditional techniques

The Japanese technique of joining metal mixtures then carving them, is called "mokume gane." Traditionally gold, silver and copper were used in mokume gane mixtures. Today, silversmiths are using modern metals, such as stainless steel, in these mixtures. In 2003, researchers developed a mixture of alloys they called "gum metal." This metal can be twisted or bent and will still spring back to its original shape.

Stainless steel

Stainless steel is a new metal which only became available to artists in the 1950s. It is an alloy of iron and carbon that avoids all **corrosion**. This cheap product can be mass produced. It has provided artists with a material that has the great advantage of being truly stainless.

◀ This stainless steel sculpture is called *The Navigators*.

🔺 A bronze figure, called *Reclining Figure*, by sculptor, Henry Moore.

Traditional metals, new techniques

Traditional metals such as bronze, silver, gold, and iron are still very popular materials with artists. New techniques with these metals are constantly being developed and explored. Artists in the 1900s used traditional metals to create sculptures that were non-realistic and unlike anything that had been seen before. Henry Moore, one of the most influential artists of the 1900s, made many such sculptures in bronze.

The Artist Speaks

"There is no background better to sculpture than the sky. There is no competition, no distraction from other solid objects."
Henry Moore, English sculptor

Bronze casting

Metal artists have found that **casting** is the best method of working with bronze. Bronze is one of the strongest materials available to the artist. It is easiest to work when it is **molten**. A process called lost wax casting is most often used to shape molten bronze. This method is used to produce all kinds of bronze works, such as large sculptures, small figurines, awards, and jewelry.

🔺 In order to get the bronze sculpture out, the mold has to be broken.

🔺 Molten bronze is carefully poured into cylinders to create the casting.

Lost wax casting

To make a casting, the artist creates the sculpture out of wax. All the details required on the finished piece are carved into the wax sculpture. A mold of the sculpture is then made out of plaster.

After the mold has hardened, molten wax is poured into it to make a hollow wax casting of the shape. Wax cylinders are attached to the mold, and the whole shape is then covered in clay and fired. This hardens the clay and melts the wax, allowing it to run out.

Molten bronze is then poured into the cylinders to fill the shape. When the bronze has hardened, the clay mold is broken off, leaving a bronze sculpture. The sculpture is then cleaned with acid and other chemicals to create a color for the surface.

🔺 The bronze sculptures change color when they are cleaned with chemicals.

Metal history

Metals have been used throughout history to make both useful and decorative objects.

The discovery of the uses of metals had a great influence on developments in history. In fact the early stages of history are named after the materials that were worked at that time. The Stone Age is the era when stone was the hardest material used. The Bronze Age followed and then the Iron Age.

Most metals in use today have been used in artworks for thousands of years. Copper was the earliest metal to be used more than 8,000 years ago. It was used for ornaments and weapons but its softness caused problems. Metal workers discovered that adding an amount of tin to the copper made bronze which is harder, so it is easier to cast and shape.

◀ This copper scroll dates from around 68–100 A.D.

Great metals traditions

There has been a huge range of traditions and styles of metalwork throughout history. In bronze artwork, perhaps the greatest are the West African Benin bronzes and the work of the Chinese Shang dynasty.

West African metal casting

In the 1300s to 1500s, very fine cast bronze sculptures were made in West Africa. These Benin bronzes show great artistic skill and individual style.

Chinese bronze

The first Bronze Age in China began in the middle of the Shang dynasty around 1500 B.C. Bronze was used for bells, mirrors, vases, bowls, cups, weapons, and the decoration of horses and chariots. The decoration on the vases, bowls, and cups consists of masks and mythical monster forms, such as dragons.

🔺 This bronze face mask was made during the Shang dynasty.

Metal treasures

Naming the most treasured metal artworks is an almost impossible task, as there are so many. Ancient Egypt and South America both have great precious metal histories. Unfortunately, most of the treasures from South America were melted down when European explorers invaded.

It is not only precious metals that should be considered as treasures. Metals such as bronze, iron, and copper have been used to create great metal artworks.

⬇ This silver bowl is called the *Gundestrup Cauldron*. It is made by a process known as Repoussé.

▶ This is the only surviving large ancient Roman bronze. It was made in 80 CE as a tribute to the military leader Marcus Aurelius.

Egyptian gold

The earliest known gold objects may date from before 6000 B.C. They are small beads that were found in graves in Egypt. A great deal of Egyptian gold artwork has been found in tombs over the past 200 years. Many of the processes they used to work gold can also be seen in images on the tomb walls.

In ancient Egypt, gold was used as a sign of power. It was used for many items of jewelry, including head ornaments, collar necklaces, rings, earrings, and bracelets.

Ancient Egyptian goldsmiths used a method called granulation in which they attached granules of gold to an object by soldering. They used this method as well as the common methods of beating and casting in molds.

⬥ The coffin of the pharaoh Tutankhamen was made around 3,500 years ago, weighs 2,488 pounds (1,128.5 kg), and is made of solid gold.

CASE STUDY
Eiffel Tower

The Eiffel Tower is a very large wrought iron tower that dominates the Paris skyline. It was designed and built by Alexandre Gustave Eiffel for the Paris World's Fair of 1889. For thousands of years metal artworks had been handmade, but in the 1850s, mass production of iron was developed. This meant building large metalworks such as the Eiffel Tower was possible.

The lower section consists of four huge arched legs. They curve inward until they meet at the top of the tower. A weather station and a television transmission antenna were later added to the top of the tower.

Eiffel Tower Statistics

Built: 1889

Material: 6,200 tons (6,300,000 kg) of iron

Original height: 984 feet (300 m)

Number of parts in the structure: 18,000

Number of rivets used: 2,500,000

Artist profile: Gustave Eiffel (1832–1923)

Gustave Eiffel's works are famous for their great craftsmanship and graceful design. Eiffel was a French engineer and builder, from a family of craftspeople and timber and coal merchants.

In 1855 he joined a company that made large items such as steam engines.

In 1858, Eiffel was put in charge of the construction of a railway bridge at Bordeaux. For a time, this was the highest bridge ever built. By 1884 his work was renowned around the world.

Eiffel became a great success and his metal structures were soon being admired. He helped the artist Auguste Bartholdi to create a giant sculpture. It was the Statue of Liberty, and it was unveiled in New York in 1886.

Where metal artists work

Metal artists usually work in a workshop. These vary greatly with the type of metal used. Precious metals artists do not require much space to work in. This is because their metals are used in small amounts to make small items. Base metals such as iron and steel alloys are used to make larger items and therefore need very different facilities.

Metals with a high **melting point** such as bronze require special furnaces to reach very high temperatures. After construction, larger objects need to be transported to the place they are to be displayed. This means that some artists may also need a yard outside their workshop.

▼ Large welded metal sculptures are often displayed outside.

CASE STUDY
Wrought iron

Working wrought iron has a long history in Europe. Iron is wrought by hammering hot iron into shape. People who work iron in this traditional way are called blacksmiths. The hammering removes any impurities that may still be in the iron after it has been heated. Blacksmiths traditionally wrought armor, weapons, and door handles for castles.

During the 1700s in Europe, wrought iron was worked with great skill to create both decorative and useful items. Later, with the development of mass production of steel, wrought iron lost popularity.

Today many artists are rediscovering this medium for their artworks as it can be worked easily in smaller workshops. Modern wrought iron workers using traditional approaches can make impressive pieces of furniture.

▶ Complicated wrought iron designs can be worked at fairly low temperatures.

Showing metal artworks

Metal artworks are shown or exhibited in galleries, parks, and museums. Where they are shown depends on their size and the types of metal used to make them. Smaller works in metal such as jewelry are often quite valuable. These are often displayed in galleries. The most valuable pieces are securely held in display cases.

Large metal artworks designed for display in city streets, public gardens, and museums are now seen all over the world. Special sculpture parks have also been established to display metal artworks. Most large metal artworks are designed for a particular space.

▼ Metal artworks can be displayed outside because the weather will not affect them greatly.

Sculpture Park: Perry Green

Perry Green is a 70 acres (28 hc) sculpture park located in Hertfordshire, England. It was the home of the famous sculptor Henry Moore. At Perry Green, huge works by Moore are permanently on display for people to visit.

Making a living as an artist

Metal artists need to make a living by selling their works at markets, through shops and galleries, or at special exhibitions.

Artists may be interested in exploring their own ideas and developing new techniques, but they also need to sell works to make a living. Most artists create stock items that sell well while also developing their new ideas.

Mokume gane

The ancient technique of mokume gane is increasing in popularity. It creates very colorful metal pieces, each of which looks different. Mokume gane means "wood grained metal" in Japanese. Recent developments have made mokume gane easier to produce, so it is being used more by metal artists to create interesting and salable items.

"The range of metal combinations and patterns is so large that each work is unique. Indeed, every new piece is a new experiment, a new adventure."
Ian Ferguson, mokume gane artist

◄ Well-made mokume gane artwork shows off colors within the metal.

Metal artists' groups

Metal artists, like many other people with a common interest, form groups to discuss issues of importance. There are as many groups as there are metals to work. These groups often have Web sites where members can display their works.

Online metal groups

Metal artists can keep up with developments in their field using the Internet, where they can also advertize their products. People from all over the world can view and buy items that they see on the Internet.

Navajo Supersmiths

Navajo silversmiths have been making jewelry for over a century. A group of them are known as the Navajo Supersmiths. They make silver and gold jewelry decorated with beautiful stones.

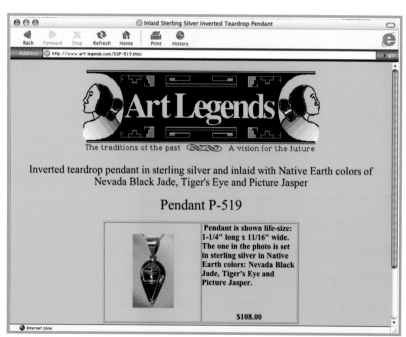

◀ Displaying metal artworks online lets visitors see entire galleries at the click of a button.

Issues for metal artists

Metal artists' groups help to share information about important issues. Health and safety is very important in metalwork as heat is involved in many of the processes. Environmental issues are also important to metal artists. Metals are obtained from the earth. They are natural resources that are limited in supply.

The Artist Speaks

"I choose to make use of recycled metal in my artworks. When a metal object is broken or unwanted it can be melted down and the metal reused. Even unwanted drink cans can be recycled into decorative items. I think this helps highlight environmental issues important today and help to conserve resources."

Janet Williams,
mixed media (junk) artist

▼ The correct safety equipment must be worn when working metal.

CASE STUDY
Cosmic Dancer

Artworks in metal have even been sent into space. In May 1993, a sculpture called *Cosmic Dancer* was sent up to the Mir Space Station to allow the cosmonauts to share their living space with artwork.

Cosmic Dancer is a small welded aluminum sculpture colored to contrast with the space station. On the space station, the sculpture was allowed to float freely and spin through the living area.

△ *Cosmic Dancer* is a complicated sculture that bends and twists back in on itself.

The Artist Speaks

"Green is associated with terrestrial plants and has calming psychological effects."
Arthur Woods, artist

Contemporary metal art in space

⬧ The Mir Space Station had its own piece of metal artwork.

Cosmic Dancer was made by Swiss American artist Arthur Woods. It measures 14 inches by 14 inches by 16 inches (35 cm by 35 cm by 40 cm) and weighs 2.2 pounds (1 kg).

The *Cosmic Dancer* project was sponsored by a group called "ars astronautica." The group want art to be included with the exploration of space.

The project was designed as a scientific experiment to test the effects of art on those living in the space station. The artist was told that the color scheme of the artwork should contrast with the Mir environment. It was designed to be a pleasing art object for the cosmonauts. It was colored green to remind the astronauts of the plants back on Earth.

PROJECT
Make a Repoussé decoration

What you need:

- a sheet of soft metal
- tracing paper
- a hammering tool
- stamping tools
- backing board (e.g. heavy card)
- a hook or cord

Repoussé decoration involves creating patterns on soft sheet metal. Simple patterns or whole pictures are created by hammering. This technique has been used for over 4,000 years.

What to do:

1. Sketch a design on tracing paper. Place the tracing paper over the metal sheet and fix it in place.

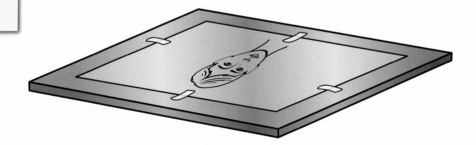

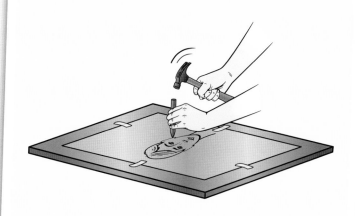

2. Using the stamping and hammering tools, copy the design onto the metal.

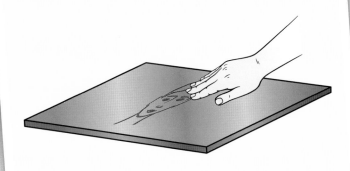

3. Examine the surface of the metal to check which areas need more work.

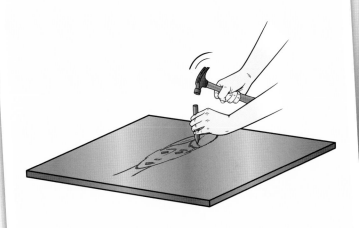

4. Go over the design and add more decoration until you are happy with it.

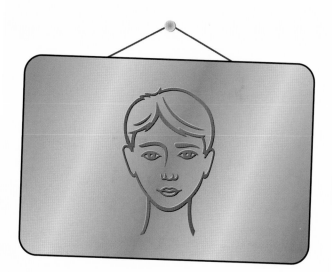

5. Add the backing board, curve the edges down to create a smooth surface, and add a hook or cord for hanging.

Metal timeline

B.C.

6000 Metal knives of copper made with blade edges hardened by hammering

5200 Egyptians extract copper from mineral deposits with fire and charcoal

3500+ Bronze metal alloy made in Mesopotamia by mixing copper and tin

3000 Silver extracted from lead ore called galena

2000 Metal working industry spreads through Europe

1500 Iron smelting began in Asia

1350 Welding iron developed in Egypt

1000 Greeks harden iron weapons using heat, Indian metalworkers make a form of steel covering for weapons

600s Metal coins issued in Asia Minor

600 Cast iron produced in China

200 Indians make a form of steel in crucibles

A.D.

around 300 Cast iron made in China

700 Iron smelting developed in Spain

1100s Iron forge developed in Spain

1300s Cast iron made in Europe

1350 Tin is used to make armor

1709 Coke-fired furnace developed in England

1740 Englishman Benjamin Huntsman rediscovers Indian crucible steel

1745 Mass production of wrought iron developed in Sweden

1791 Titanium discovered

1877 Modern electric arc welding process developed

1886 Commercial process for smelting aluminum discovered

1925 Titanium obtained in pure form

1993 First metal artwork in space

2003 New bendy "gum metal" alloy devised

alloys mixtures of metals

arc welding a process of heating metal for joining by using large electric currents

bauxite ore in which aluminum is found

casting shaping by pouring liquid into a mold

chemicals substances with a particular composition of atoms

corrosion chemical reaction such as rusting

crystalline substance with a crystal structure

igneous formed from molten material

lustrous shines by reflecting light

medium material used

melting point temperature at which a chemical turns from solid to liquid

mercury heavy, silvery metal that is liquid at normal temperatures

molten liquid form, melted material

ore natural form in which metals are found

properties characteristics that make up a material

riveting a method of fastening metal using a metal pin or bolt

titanium metal that resembles iron that is very strong but also very light

welding joining of metals by heating, to fuse pieces together

Index